FAITH WORKS NOW

By Gary McSpadden

Gary McSpadden

Founding Pastor of Faith and Wisdom Church

2008–2020

Scripture quotations are taken from the NKJV & KJV
ISBN: 979-8-218-78665-6
Printed in the United States of America.

Dedication

To all the people who do not know Christ, that their hearts would be changed and have a closer walk with their lord and savior Jesus Christ, and faith would be instilled in them.

— Carol McSpadden

Foreword

A book inspired through the scriptures from the Bible and the Anointing of the Holy Spirit that inspired Gary McSpadden to write these proclamations so that you can live a daily life of **Faith**, that can **strengthen** you to become a **strong** and fulfilled **believer** in Christ!

Read these proclamations every day. Memorize the scriptures and let your **Faith** become a daily walk with the Lord!

He will make you strong in your belief that God can do all things for those who believe and walk with Him.

Let Christ be first in your life! He cares and loves you! **Believe**, have **Faith** and miracles will begin to happen!

— *Carol McSpadden*

Table of Contents

FAITH WORKS

THERE ARE 4 BASICS TO WALKING IN FAITH.

1.   Hearing. This is not a past tense use of the word but a present tense usage.
Faith keeps on hearing and hearing and hearing over and over again.

> *Romans 10:17 "Now faith comes by hearing and hearing by the Word of God."*

God honors faith! Faith is important to God.

2.   Being persuaded. Being convinced. Like Abraham who, after hearing God's promise, exhibited no doubt at all.

> *Romans 4:20 – 21, "he did not waver at the promise of God through unbelief, but was strengthened in faith, giving glory to God. (21) and being fully convinced that what He had promised He was also able to perform."*

3. **Expecting.** If we walk in faith, we are expecting! If you are not expecting, you are not in faith. Those who expect nothing, will always get what they expect…nothing! Faith expects what God promised because faith hears what God says and is convinced that it will come. When we walk in faith, we expect God to do exactly what He promised.

4. **Preparing.** Are you getting ready to receive the thing for which you are believing? To receive all that God wants to give to you, you must press in, prepare and not draw back. You must live in a faith filled state of expectation and preparation.

> *Hebrews 10:38 says, "Now the just shall live by faith: but if any man draw back, My soul shall have no pleasure in him."*

YOU NEED EXPECTANT FAITH

One of the great definitions of faith is found in Hebrews.

> *"Now faith is the substance of things hoped for, the evidence of things not seen." (Hebrews 11:1, KJV)*

Here is a different translation for this scripture… *"Being persuaded is the foundation for the things I expect. It is the proof of what I am expecting, even though I don't yet see it."*

There is some misunderstanding of the word hope used in Hebrews 11:1. In our language, the word hope is sometimes equal to the word wish. But to wish for something is not to expect it. You hope for money to pay the obligation, but faith in God is the assurance that you will have the money when you need it, even if you don't see it yet. You hope that you will have the physical strength and healing, but faith says, *"By His stripes I am healed,"* You see, faith says the same thing the Word of God says!

TESTS OF YOUR FAITH

TEST #1. WILL YOU TRUST GOD WITH THE POSSESSIONS HE HAS GIVEN YOU?

Will you trust God with your possessions? Sometimes we say we are willing to give up everything _for_ the Lord, but are we willing to give it up _to_ the Lord? There's a big difference. When you turn your heart over to God, your possessions will follow.

TEST #2. WILL YOU TRUST GOD WITH HIS PURPOSES FOR YOU?

Understanding and doing the will of God requires three simple steps:

1.   Finding the will of God.

2.   Following the will of God.

3.   Finishing the will of God.

Faith is not simply obeying in spite of the evidence…it is obeying in spite of consequences. It is obeying whether or not we understand the purpose of it all. It is simply obeying God!

God told Abraham to sacrifice his son. This was the most difficult decision he had ever made, but faith moves our hearts in God's direction. Abraham was fully persuaded expecting the God he trusted to provide everything he needed to fulfill the plan. He didn't know what the plan was, but he knew God was able to perform on His promise. You may not know how or when…but you must continue to trust the God of the purpose! Will you trust Him with the purpose He has for you?

TEST #3. WILL YOU TRUST GOD WITH THE PROMISES HE HAS SPOKEN?

With your faith, working from hearing the Word, you can expect God to fulfill every promise He has made. You have the creative mechanism that allows you to achieve anything you can believe for. If God promised it, there is nothing that is impossible to you! So, begin to walk in your God given authority!

The devil will keep showing up at your door because you possess something that he desperately wants...he wants you! He wants to rule your life...But Jesus defeated Satan, and we have been restored to our rightful place of authority. We are joint heirs with Him. Every time the enemy tries to attack you, consider it an opportunity to exercise your power over him by faith in the Word.

You have authority! *Matthew 16:19 says, "And I will give you the keys of the Kingdom of Heaven, and whatever you bind on Earth will be bound in Heaven, and whatever you loose on Earth will be loosed in Heaven."* I want to challenge you to begin making demands (begin asking for the impossible) in Jesus' name.

John 14:13 – 14 says, "And whatsoever ye shall ask in My name, I will do it, that the Father may be glorified in the Son. If you shall ask anything in my name I will do it." Will you trust God with the possessions He has given? Will you trust Him with the purpose He has for you? Will you trust God with the promises He has spoken for you?

DAILY FAITH PROCLAMATIONS

I challenge you to speak and proclaim the Word of God over your life every day. Choose the proclamations that relate to the needs in your personal life and begin to speak them out. I also encourage you to study the scriptures that accompany each proclamation and begin to memorize God's Word. Speak these scriptures daily and watch the Word of God help you in your everyday decisions and choices. When you attach your faith to the Word of God that you are speaking, you can begin to expect miracles in your life starting today. So, let's proclaim the Word and expect God to perform His promises.

PROCLAMATION #1

"IN THE NAME OF JESUS, I COMMAND EVERY EVIL HAND POINTED AT MY DESTINY TO WITHER AND DIE."

> *John 10:10, "The thief cometh not, but for to steal, and kill, and to destroy: I (Jesus) am come that they might have life, and that they might have it more abundantly."*

PROCLAMATION #2

"I COMMAND EVERY ENEMY THAT WOULD STOP GOD'S PLANNED PROGRESS IN MY LIFE TO BECOME CONFUSED AND BE DEFEATED IN THE NAME OF JESUS."

> *Isaiah 54:17, "No weapon formed against you shall prosper and every tongue that shall rise against you in judgment you shall condemn. This is the heritage of the servants of the Lord, and their righteousness is from me, says the Lord."*

PROCLAMATION #3
"I COMMAND THE EVIL POWER OF CURSES AND WITCHCRAFT TO DIE IN THE NAME OF JESUS'

> *2 CORINTHIANS 5:17, "What this means is that those who become Christians become new persons. They are not the same anymore, for the old life is gone. A new life has begun!"*

PROCLAMATION #4
"IN THE NAME OF JESUS, I CALL MY ENTIRE FAMILY SAVED, HEALED, FILLED WITH PEACE AND IN THE SERVICE OF THE LORD."

> *Joshua 24:1, "And if it seems evil to you to serve the LORD, choose for yourselves this day whom you will serve, whether the gods which your fathers served*

that were on the other side of the River, or the gods of the Amorites, in whose land you dwell. But as for me and my house, we will serve the LORD."

PROCLAMATION #5

"I COMMAND EVERY ANGEL ASSIGNED TO MY LIFE TO MOVE IMMEDIATELY TO YOUR PLACE OF SERVICE, PROTECTION AND THE COMPLETION OF EVERY DETAIL OF YOUR ASSIGNMENT...ANGELS OF BREAKTHROUGH, ENCAMP AROUND ME AND RELEASE GOD'S FULL AND PERFECT BLESSINGS TO ME, IN THE NAME OF JESUS."

Psalm 91: 9 – 12, "For you have made the LORD my refuge. Even the Most High, your dwelling place. No evil will befall you, nor will any plague come near your tent. For He will give His angels charge concerning you, to guard you in all your ways. They will bear you up in their hands, that you do not strike your foot against a stone."

PROCLAMATION #6

"HOLY SPIRIT OF GOD, ARISE WITHIN ME AND ANOINT AND PROMOTE ME TO SERVE YOU...HELP ME TO BUILD UP AND INCREASE YOUR KINGDOM AND DO YOUR PERFECT WILL, IN THE NAME OF JESUS."

Zechariah 4:6," ...not by might nor by power, but my Spirit (my anointing) saith the Lord of Hosts."

PROCLAMATION #7

"IN THE NAME OF JESUS, I COMMAND EVERY ARROW OF SICKNESS, DISEASE AND UNTIMELY DEATH, THAT HAS EVER BEEN PROGRAMMED INTO MY BODY BY SATAN'S FORCES...BE DEFEATED AND DESTROYED NOW!"

1 Peter 2:24, "He Himself bore our sins in His body on the tree, so that we might die to sins and live for righteousness: by His wounds you have been healed."

PROCLAMATION #8

"ACCORDING TO MY FAITH, AND IN THE NAME OF JESUS...I COMMAND THE RIVER HARBORING ALL MY BLESSINGS...BE RELEASED INTO MY LIFE NOW!"

Deuteronomy 28:1 – 2, "If you fully obey the LORD your God and carefully follow all His commands I give you today, the LORD your God will set you high above all nations on earth. All these blessings will come upon you and accompany you if you obey the LORD your God."

PROCLAMATION #9

"I COMMIT TO RIGHTEOUS FAITHFULNESS IN ALL MY FINANCIAL MATTERS...I PULL DOWN EVERY STRONGHOLD OF POVERTY. I CALL EVERY BILL PAID... EVERY NEED MET AND EVERY DEBT ELIMINATED, IN THE NAME OF JESUS."

Proverbs 10:22, "The blessing of the Lord makes one rich, and He adds no sorrow with it."

Luke 6:38, "Give, and it shall be given unto you: good measure, pressed down, and shaken together, and running over, shall men give into your bosom. For with the same measure that ye mete withal it shall be measured to you again."

DESTINY

Chapter 1

PROCLAMATION #1
"IN THE NAME OF JESUS, I COMMAND EVERY EVIL HAND POINTED AT MY DESTINY TO WITHER AND DIE."

Your destiny is not a matter of chance, IT IS a matter of choice.

If you could do anything you wanted with your life, what would it be? Instead of letting the future just happen to you...instead of letting yourself be battered and controlled by "random" events, begin speaking the Word of God into your life with faith and expectation.

> *John 10:10, "The thief cometh not, but for to steal, and to kill, and to destroy: I (Jesus) am come that they might have life, and that they might have it more abundantly.*

REFUSE TO ALLOW SATAN TO STEAL YOUR DESTINY.

Do not let the enemy of your soul steal your promise and destiny, kill your dreams and visions, and finally destroy your purpose…You are a creation of God. You have been lovingly, carefully designed and created by the hand of God. You have a God given destiny. Before the foundation of time, God knew you and He has a purpose for your life. You are a person of destiny. You are not an accident. The Lord gave you an eternally powerful message in Jeremiah.

> *Jeremiah 1:4 – 5, "Before you were born I set you apart and appointed you as my spokesman to the world."*

SATAN HATES YOU BECAUSE OF WHAT YOU HAVE BEEN PURPOSED TO ACCOMPLISH.

Satan hates everything God represents. He despises life…your life. He especially despises what your life can be and what you can do when purposed and empowered by the Spirit of God. Remember these words.

You are…
1.	A child of God
2.	A joint heir with Christ
3.	A temple…the dwelling place of God

I am here to proclaim to you that <u>YOU</u> are a child of the Most High God and He has given you a great destiny! By faith, it is time for you to take control of your destiny.

BELIEVE WHAT GOD'S WORD SAYS ABOUT YOU.

> ***Psalm 139: 13 – 14: "For you created my inmost being: you knit me together in my Mother's womb. I praise you because I am fearfully and wonderfully made; your works are wonderful, I know that full well."***

You are created in the image of God! God says that you have great value and you are not inferior to anyone. Remember that you were God's idea and God does not make mistakes. You have access to every promise of God and nothing is impossible to you when you believe and speak the Word of God over your life. Satan is alarmed because he knows you possess the mighty power of God and that you will use it against him!

REFUSE TO LISTEN TO THE VOICES OF DOUBT.

Determine to walk away from those who try to discourage you. Make certain that you avoid negative voices, people, places, things and habits. Never give in and never, never, never give up. Refuse to hear the doubters. Refuse to allow anyone else but Christ to sit in the driver's seat of your life. When you give God His place on the throne of your life, you have begun to fulfill your destiny.

PURSUE YOUR DESTINY WITH DETERMINATION.

So how do you find your destiny? Your destiny is revealed when you find your purpose. Your destiny is what God sent you here to do. Your destiny is the reason you were born...and you were born to be remarkable. Your destiny is not something you wait for, it is something you must pursue. Pursue your purpose by studying the Word of God. In His Word you will find His will. Remember, God made no one else in the world exactly like you. The great Creator personally designed and made you the way you are. He has a purpose and a destiny that is yours and yours alone.

BELIEVE AND EXPECT EVERY BLESSING THAT GOD HAS PROMISED YOU.

You will be blessed when you diligently pursue your divine destiny in obedience to God's Word. Look at Deuteronomy 28…

Deuteronomy 28 1 – 6: "You must completely obey the Lord your God, and you must carefully follow all His commands I am giving you today. Then the Lord your God will make you greater than any other nation on earth. Obey the Lord your God so that all these blessings will come and stay with you: You will be blessed in the city and blessed in the country. Your children will be blessed, as well as your crops; your herds will be blessed with calves and your flocks with lambs. Your basket and your kitchen will be blessed. You will be blessed when you come in and when you go out."

DO NOT BACK DOWN!

Now with God as your backup force, it is up to you to aggressively deal with destiny killing forces that will try to destroy you. Show these forces no mercy. Refuse to tolerate them. As a believer, you have complete power and authority over all the works of the enemy! God has begun a good work in you, and He is going to continue this work and you will see mighty results through what He will do through you. Your destiny is by His design.

> **Philippians 1:6: "He who has begun a good work in you will carry it on to completion until the day of Christ Jesus."**

Enemies

Chapter 2

PROCLAMATION #2
"I COMMAND EVERY ENEMY THAT
WOULD STOP GOD'S PLANNED
PROGRESS IN MY LIFE TO BECOME
CONFUSED AND BE DEFEATED, IN THE
NAME OF JESUS."

REFUSE TO LET ENEMIES STOP YOUR PROGRESS.

Problems may surround you…sickness may gather against you together with all its relatives…worry and all its friends will try to defeat you…evil spirits will come against you! Do not be afraid of their terror. Refuse to be moved…stand strong. You are established in righteousness.

Isaiah 54:17, "No weapon that is formed against you shall prosper and every tongue that shall rise against you in judgment you shall condemn. This is the heritage of the servants of the Lord, and their righteousness is from me, says the Lord."

YOU HAVE MANY ENEMIES

I am sure you already know that the devil is your biggest enemy...but failure, sin, and worry are enemies. The fact is, anything that opposes, challenges, and tries to destroy you is your enemy. Unfruitfulness, poverty, sickness, disease, bitterness, and uncontrolled anger are all your enemies because they oppose the purpose of God in your life. These enemies gather together against you without God's will or consent. They cannot gather in success. They are destined to fall. They cannot overcome you. You are victorious through the power of Christ... and no weapon designed for your destruction shall be able to stand.

1 Corinthians 15:57, "But thanks be to God that gives us the victory through our Lord Jesus Christ!"

YOU ARE AN OVERCOMER.

It is through the power of Jesus Christ that we can have victory over sin, over Satan, victory over peer-pressure, victory over our problems, victory over low self-esteem, victory over drugs and alcohol, victory over obstacles, victory over stumbling blocks, victory over adverse circumstances and victory over setbacks. When Jesus Christ died on the cross for our sins and rose from the dead with all power in His hands, He also made us victorious over every circumstance.

1 John 5: 4 – 5 "Whatsoever is born of God overcometh the World: and this is the victory that overcometh the World, even our faith. Who is he that overcometh the World, but he that believeth that Jesus is the Son of God?"

Ephesians 1: 20 – 21, "Which He worked in Christ when He raised Him from the dead and seated Him at His right hand in the Heavenly places, far above all principality and power and might and dominion, and every name that is named, not only in this age but also in that which is to come."

YOU ARE A VICTORIOUS WARRIOR.

We are victorious in battle because we are children of God and joint heirs with Jesus. Jesus is on our side. Because of who we are in Christ, we will walk onto the battlefield with a victorious attitude. But we must now put on the Whole Armor of God.

Ephesians 6:10 – 17, "Finally, my brethren, be strong in the Lord and in the power of His might. Put on the whole armor of God, that you may be able to stand against the wiles of the devil. For we do not wrestle against flesh and blood, but against principalities, against powers, against the rulers of the darkness of this age, against spiritual hosts of wickedness in the Heavenly places. Therefore take up the whole armor of God, that you may be able to withstand in the evil day, and having done all, to stand. And stand therefore, having girded your waist with truth, and having put on the breastplate of righteousness, and having shod your feet with the preparation of the gospel of peace; above all, taking the shield of faith with which you will be able to quench all the fiery darts of the wicked one. And take the helmet of salvation, and the sword of the Spirit, which is in the Word of God."

Twice in this passage of scripture we are exhorted by the Word to put on the whole armor of God.

1.   First of all, it must be emphasized how important it is to put on the *whole* armor. If we fail to put on just one piece of the armor, we leave ourselves vulnerable to the enemy's attack. Satan's not a nice guy. He won't hesitate to kick you when you're down. He will always look for weaknesses in you and will do his best to exploit them. When you put on the whole armor, you'll be ready to handle any and every attack of the enemy.

2.   The second thing, which needs to be emphasized, is the fact that this armor is not our armor, but it is God's armor. Here is an amazing fact…we get to use God's Armor. It is not something which we have fabricated ourselves, but it is something, which is supplied to us from the Hand of God. The only time you will suffer defeat is when you fail to put on the whole armor of God. Put it on through prayer and commitment to God daily. Take hold of the things that He has given us to use.

2 Corinthians 10: 4 – 6, "For the weapons of our warfare are not carnal but mighty in God for pulling down strongholds, casting down arguments and every high thing that exalts itself against the knowledge of God, bringing every thought into captivity to the obedience of Christ, and being ready to punish all disobedience when your obedience is fulfilled."

Enemies

Chapter 3

PROCLAMATION #3
"I COMMAND THE EVIL POWER OF CURSES
AND WITCHCRAFT TO DIE, IN THE NAME OF JESUS."

GENERATIONAL CURSES MUST GO!

When we hear of generational curses that might be attached to your lives, we are not helpless! We are only helpless when we are ignorant of what is taking place in our lives. When we identify them, we have an opportunity to confess the sin and break the curse just as Nehemiah did. Here is what he said…

> *Nehemiah 1: 5 – 7, "I pray, LORD God of Heaven, O great and awesome God, You who keep Your covenant and mercy with those who love You and observe Your*

commandments. Please let your ear be attentive and your eyes open, that You may hear the prayer of Your servant which I pray before You now, day and night, for the children of Israel Your servants, and confess the sins of the children of Israel which we have sinned against You. Both my Father's house and I have sinned. We have acted very corruptly against You, and have not kept the commandments, the statutes, nor the ordinances which You commanded Your servant Moses."

What Nehemiah confessed here was the generational sin of his relatives and ancestors, and he did this in order to break the curse of sin both in his own life and in the life of his descendants. Nehemiah was basically saying, "Lord, I remember your admonition about generational sin, but I also remember You saying that You are a forgiving God." There are numerous sinful behavioral patterns and sins that can be passed on through the generations such as: Divorce, Addictions, Sexual Sins, Emotional Disorders, Depression, Bitterness, Negativity, Prejudice, Poverty, Failure, and Worry.

YOU HAVE A NEW DNA.

Being in Christ…being a new creation gives a totally different meaning to your genetic DNA. If you are in Christ and He in you, you are no longer under the curse of sin and death. And so, you are no longer under the curse of cancer, heart disease, stroke, diabetes, Alzheimer's, paralysis or anything else that threatens to steal, kill and destroy your life. It does not matter that your Mother, or Father, or Grandmother, or Uncle, or cousin—had these diseases. You are a new creation, and you have the blood of Jesus Christ flowing through your veins, you are free from the sins and sicknesses of the generations that came before you.

When you are born into the family of God you have a new bloodline. At the point of your spiritual rebirth there is a definite change in your DNA…you have a new generic heritage. Since your Father God loves unconditionally, you are now able to love in the same manner. Since He is a giver, you are now a giver too. It seems that everything on earth has a likeness to something in Heaven and so; we have a likeness to God. He made us in His image.

Genesis 1:26 says, "Then God said, Let us make man in our image, in our likeness…"

He gave us His likeness and His nature! Your new DNA is God's Divine Nature Applied to your life. Paul tells us in…

> **2 Corinthians 5:17, "What this means is that those who become Christians become new persons. They are not the same anymore, for the old life is gone. A new life has begun!"**

Our first birth was from Heaven to earth, but our second birth is from earth back to Heaven. You have a different Father. You are now part of a new family lineage that is Spiritual and eternal. We possess eternal cellular organisms that are not of this World…we came from a place called Heaven before we ever appeared here on earth. Do not embrace the idea that because some family member had a disease, which you are required to accept and believe you too will suffer. Do not believe that it is inevitable. Jesus took stripes on His back for you and by His stripes you are healed! You have the bloodline of a new family…a new heritage. You are a child of God. If you are in Jesus Christ, you have been born again. You have been made a new creation. You have a new DNA! Now that you have been made aware of this fact, you can begin to use the authority that has been given to you. It's time to stand up against the enemy because you are free!

REFUSE TO ALLOW CURSES TO RENDER YOU HELPLESS.

The Bible says in…

> *1 John 1:9, "If we confess our sin, He is faithful and just to forgive us our sin and to cleanse us from all unrighteousness."*

Breaking a generational curse comes through faith, confession and repentance. As the Bible says, we must confess "our" sins, as well as the sins of our ancestors. We must then repent of those sins. The good news is this, that when we confess those sins and turn away from them, we break the curse!

It's time for you to break the curse of sin in your life. If you can identify sins in your life that are the result of a wrong behavior passed down through the generations, then confess those sins and ask for forgiveness. Then turn from those sins and you will break the cycle of those sins in your family line.

Please, use all your strength and use the following prayer points: You can pray in this manner…

1. In the name of *Jesus*, I refuse to allow my past to determine my future.

2. I take authority over all curses in my life, in the name of *Jesus*.

3. In the name of *Jesus*, I command the release and destruction of any curse that is the result of my disobedience, and I declare that I will live in full obedience to the Word of God.

4. In the name of *Jesus*, I command any demon attached to any curse upon my life to depart from me now.

5. Let all curses against me be converted to blessing, in the name of *Jesus*.

6. I say to every curse…be broken, in the name of *Jesus*.

I speak this in *Jesus* Name…

Every curse of mental and physical sickness be broken!
Every curse of failure and defeat be broken!
Every curse of poverty be broken!
Every curse of family break-up be broken!
Every curse of addiction be broken!
Every curse of oppression be broken!
Every curse of bad reputation be broken! Every curse of personal destruction or suicide be broken!

I command every curse upon my life…be destroyed today in the name of *Jesus*!

Family

Chapter 4

PROCLAMATION #4
*"IN THE NAME OF JESUS, I CALL MY
ENTIRE FAMILY SAVED, HEALED,
FILLED WITH PEACE AND IN THE
SERVICE OF THE LORD."*

GOD'S DESIRE FOR YOU.

God wants you to have peace, healing and
salvation for your family. To have the peace of
God you must break the strongholds that the
devil has placed in the lives of your family. You
will face a real battle as you begin to tear down
these strongholds. But with the power of faith
and the Word of God at your disposal these
strongholds will be destroyed.

The devil knows this, but he is a crafty and
cunning creature. He will try to deepen his
claws in your family. Remember, your family is
not the first family to be attacked by the
devil. He began with the first family, Adam and
Eve. His mission is simple and always the

same. Divide and conquer: divide the parents, divide the children. He will attack your family and make you want to quit. You must resist him. This scripture is a key to your victory.

> **James 4:7 "Submit yourselves, then, to God. Resist the devil and he will flee from you."**

If your family is to be victorious, there are some strongholds that you need to recognize.

1.   *SELFISHNESS.*

One stronghold that the devil uses against the family is the stronghold of selfishness. If the devil can get you to believe that you need to be looking out for number one and think only of pleasing yourself first, then he has you in his grip. This is what Eve did. Satan convinced her that she would be better off if she didn't listen to Adam, and so she did it her own way. Thinking of only yourself is a stronghold that the devil places in the lives of the family. It creates disorder. It creates disunity. You must put others first.

2. *REBELLION.*

Cain and Able were the first children on this earth. Cain rebelled against God and God rebuked him. When rebellion is allowed to run rampant there is chaos. When a parent rebels against God's command there is chaos. When children rebel against parents there is chaos. This is Satan's tool. He knows that if he can keep your family in chaos and keep your life in chaos then he knows he can keep your mind on your problems more than on your God. You must break the stronghold of rebellion. Break it first in your own life and then, with God's help you will break the rebellion in your family. If you have never claimed your Biblical authority as a parent, you must begin today.

3. *UNRESOLVED ANGER.*

The last thing we see that happened is Cain got angry. We are told in the book of James, ***"not to give place to the devil".*** Cain was so angry with God and his brother that he killed him. Anger makes us say things that under normal circumstances we would never say. Anger blinds us and causes us to feel self-pity. It causes us to feel that the whole world is against us. We become blinded when we allow the devil to build the stronghold of anger in our families.

There are some steps to breaking the strongholds in your family.

1. <u>RECOGNIZE THAT YOU ARE FIGHTING A SPIRITUAL BATTLE.</u>

Ephesians 6:12, "For we wrestle not against flesh and blood, but against principalities, powers, against the rulers of the darkness of this world, against spiritual wickedness in high places."

2. <u>ENSURE YOUR FOUNDATION.</u>

Let your children know who is the Lord of your house and show them by the way you live.

Joshua 24:1, "And if it seems evil to you to serve the LORD, choose for yourselves this day whom you will serve, whether the gods which your fathers served that were on the other side of the River, or the gods of the Amorites, in whose land you dwell. But as for me and my house, we will serve the LORD."

It is so important that we make God our foundation so that he can stabilize the family and bring order to the home. If you want to break these things that are tearing down your family then you make a decision today. "As for me and my house we will serve the Lord". And you stand up to the enemy no matter what you face.

3. *BUILD A STRONG MARRIAGE.*

Strength lies in unity—Wives submit to your Husband.

> **Ephesians 5:22, "Wives, submit to your own husbands, as to the Lord."**

Husbands sacrifice for your wife.

> **Ephesians 5:25, "Husbands. Love your wives, just as Christ also loved the church and gave Himself for her."**

A strong marriage is partnering together to bring glory to the Lord.

Angels

Chapter 5

PROCLAMATION #5
*"I COMMAND EVERY ANGEL ASSIGNED TO
MY LIFE TO MOVE IMMEDIATELY TO YOUR
PLACE OF SERVICE, PROTECTION AND
THE COMPLETION OF EVERY DETAIL OF
YOUR ASSIGNMENT...ANGELS OF
BREAKTHROUGH, ENCAMP AROUND ME
AND RELEASE GOD'S FULL AND PERFECT
BLESSINGS TO ME, IN THE NAME OF
JESUS."*

There are many things about God's angels
that we need to know.

1. *ANGELS ARE MIGHTY IN*
    STRENGTH.

    Psalm 103:20, "Bless the LORD,
    you His angels, mighty in strength,
    who perform His word obeying the
    voice of His word!

2 Peter 2:11, "...whereas angels who are greater in might and power..." Holy angels (those loyal to God) are ministers of the Lord."

2.   ANGELS GUARD AND PROTECT.

Psalm 91: 9 – 12, "For you have made the LORD, my refuge, Even the Most High, your dwelling place. No evil will befall you, nor will any plague come near your tent. For He will give His angels charge concerning you, to guard you in all your ways. They will bear you up in their hands, that you do not strike your foot against a stone.

3.   ANGELS ARE SERVANTS.

Hebrews 1:14, "Are not all angels ministering spirits sent to SERVE those who will inherit salvation? They are around to help us, as servants of the mighty God. They are to us God's special messengers of His love."

In fact, the Greek word *angelos* has its basic meaning rooted in the word "messenger". One of the things they do is to carry God's Word to people as found in the Christmas story in

> **Luke 1:26 – 28. *"And in the sixth month the angel Gabriel was sent from God unto a city of Galilee, named Nazareth. To a virgin espoused to a man whose name was Joseph, of the house of David: and the virgin's name was Mary. And the angel came in unto her, and said, Hail, thou that art highly favored, the Lord is with thee: blessed are thou among women."***

This is a great comfort, especially for those who are undergoing hard times. You may not be able to see them, but could there be angels helping out in your life, serving, clearing the way, ministering to you in your time of need?

4. ANGELS MINISTER TO GOD'S PEOPLE.

Hebrews 1:14, "But to which of the angels has He ever said, "Sit as my right hand, until I make your enemies a footstool for your feet"? Are they not all ministering spirits, sent out to render service for the sake of those who will inherit salvation?"

5. ANGELS REJOICE WHEN ONE SINNER REPENTS.

Luke 15: 7, 10, "I tell you that in the same way, there will be more joy in heaven over one sinner who repents than over ninety-nine righteous persons who need no repentance...I tell you, there is joy in the presence of the angels of God over one sinner who repents."

Anointing

Chapter 6

PROCLAMATION #6

"HOLY SPIRIT OF GOD, ARISE WITHIN ME ANOINT AND PROMOTE ME TO SERVE YOU...HELP ME TO BUILD UP AND INCREASE YOUR KINGDOM AND DO YOUR PERFECT WILL, IN THE NAME OF JESUS."

There will be times when you will struggle with whether or not God is with you or not. In our darkest hours and in our weakest moments the enemy comes in to devour our faith, steal our strength, and destroy us. But the truth is that in our darkest hour, in our weakest moments, there is a fresh anointing.

1. *THE ANOINTING AUTHORIZES YOU AND SETS YOU APART.*

The anointing speaks of enduement, impartation and empowering for a particular work in the Kingdom of God.

Isaiah 61:1, "The Spirit of the Sovereign Lord is on me, because the Lord has anointed me to preach good news to the poor. He has sent me to bind up the brokenhearted, to proclaim freedom for the captives and release from darkness for the prisoners...to comfort all who mourn, to bestow on them a crown of beauty instead of ashes, the oil of gladness instead of mourning, and a garment of praise instead of a spirit of despair."

2. THE ANOINTING IS THE POWER OF GOD AT WORK IN YOU.

1 John 2:20, "But you have an anointing from the Holy One, and all of you know the truth".

1 John 2: 27, "As for you, the anointing you received from Him remains in you, and you do not need anyone to teach you. But as His anointing teaches you about all things and as that anointing is real, not counterfeit – just as it has taught you, remain in Him".

The anointing of the Holy Ghost is the power of God at work in you to do the work of God.

> **Zechariah 4:6, "…not by might nor by power, but by my Spirit (my anointing) saith the Lord of Hosts".**

Sickness and Disease

Chapter 7

PROCLAMATION #7
"IN THE NAME OF JESUS, I COMMAND
EVERY ARROW OF SICKNESS, DISEASE
AND UNTIMELY DEATH, THAT HAS EVER
BEEN PROGRAMMED INTO MY BODY BY
SATAN'S FORCES,...BE DEFEATED AND
DESTROYED NOW"!

HEALING IS GOD'S WILL FOR YOU.

Healing is not just something that God "does", no, it's much more than that. Healing is part of God's very nature. **"I AM the Lord who heals you."**

Remember that you serve a God who has declared His intent towards you is *"Not (to) bring on you and diseases... (but to be) the Lord who heals you"*.

God is for us, not against us, in the matter of healing.

> *Exodus 15: 26, (God) said, "If you listen carefully to the voice of the LORD your God and do what is right in His eyes, if you pay attention to His commands and keep all His decrees, I will not bring on you any of the diseases I brought on the Egyptians, for I am the LORD, who heals you".*

HE IS JEHOVAH-RAPHA...THE LORD WHO HEALS YOU.

God identifies Himself to Israel in a variety of names and ways. Here He reveals Himself to His people as *"Jehovah-Rapha"* ...the Lord who heals you. God's spiritual healing power extends to ALL our diseases and infirmities.

> *Psalm 103: 2, 3, "Praise the LORD O my soul, and forget not all His benefits, who forgives all your sins and heals all your diseases."*

Remember that Jesus died for both our sins and our sickness.

Isaiah 53:5, "But He was pierced for our transgressions, He was crushed for our iniquities, the punishment that brought us peace was upon Him, and by His wounds we are healed."

It was Jesus' willingness to offer Himself up to a death on the Cross that saves us from our sins. But the very same tormented body of Jesus, in His scourging and crucifixion, purchased for us the blessing of divine healing...*By His stripes you have been healed."*

1 Peter 2:24, "He Himself bore our sins in His body on the tree, so that we might die to sins and live for righteousness, by His wounds you have been healed."

Notice the difference in the verb tenses used by Isaiah and Peter. Isaiah, living seven centuries before Christ, seeing the stripes placed on the body of the Messiah, spoke prophetically and said, *"By His wounds <u>we are</u> healed."*

The Apostle Peter, looking back to Christ's historical death and resurrection, declared, *"By His wounds <u>you have been</u> healed."*

Jesus cried out from the Cross, *"It is finished!"* Sin has been overcome. Sickness has been overcome. The Cross of Jesus Christ has conquered both sin and sickness. So you can believe and speak out this proclamation today.

Blessings

Chapter 8

PROCLAMATION #8
"ACCORDING TO MY FAITH, AND IN THE NAME OF JESUS...I COMMAND THE RIVER HARBORING ALL MY BLESSINGS...BE RELEASED INTO MY LIFE NOW!"

GOD HAS MADE A COVENANT OF BLESSING WITH YOU.

It's one thing to be blessed in a place, it's another to be in the Blessing Place. You can be blessed wherever you are, but to live in the place of blessing is where God wants us. God made a covenant with Abraham...

1.   It was irrevocable.
2.   It was eternal.
3.   It could be inherited.

God's covenant began with Abraham and was finished at a place called Calvary. Do you believe God's Blessings are available to every one of us? Do you believe His promises are true? If He said it in His Word, do you believe that it will come to pass?

Galatians 3:29, says this, "***And now that you belong to Christ, you are the true children of Abraham."***

You see, the blessings of God are ours. God made the covenant with Abraham and then God sealed that covenant with the Cross, the sacrifice and the resurrection of God's only Son, Jesus Christ. If we choose to live in the place of blessing, we must live there by faith. This is the only way we can reside in a place where God can do what He has already promised and provided. It's when we refuse to live by faith that we remove ourselves from residing in the place of God's continual blessings.

Deuteronomy 28:1 -2, "If you fully obey the Lord your God and carefully follow all His commands I give you today, the Lord your God will set you high above all the nations on earth. All these blessings will come upon you and accompany you if you obey the LORD your God."

Do you really believe that all the promises of God belong to you? If God promised you the covenant of Blessing…salvation, healing, health, prosperity, joy, peace, Heaven, it's all mine and it's all yours. We can claim it. The Blessing Place is a wonderful place to live, but we can only get to this place by traveling the road of real true faith.

So, speak this out today, "God I'm going to do whatever Your Word says to do."
If You tell me to give a tenth, Lord, I'm going to do it.

If You tell me that You'll bless me when I give my offerings, I'm going to do it.
If You tell me that You're going to bless my family with health and prosperity when I walk in Your Will, I will do it.

If You tell me that You are going to fill my heart with joy and peace as I hide Your Word in my heart, I'm going to do it.

If You tell me You're going to keep me from temptation and that You're going to walk with me every day as I pray, I'm going to do it. As you begin speaking and living out these words on a daily basis, you will begin to experience life in the Blessing Place.

Increases

Chapter 9

PROCLAMATION #9
*"I COMMIT TO RIGHTEOUS FAITHFULNESS
IN ALL MY FINANCIAL MATTERS...I PULL
DOWN EVERY STRONGHOLD OF POVERTY.
I CALL ALL MY BILLS PAID...EVERY NEED
MET AND EVERY DEBT ELIMINATED, IN THE
NAME OF JESUS."*

THE BLESSING OF INCREASE IS PROMISED TO THOSE WHO ARE OBEDIENT.

> *Proverbs 10:22 The blessing of
> the Lord makes one rich, and He
> adds no sorrow with it."*

*Joshua 1:8 "This book of the law
shall not depart out of thy mouth,
but thou shalt meditate therein day
and night, that thou mayest observe
to do according to all that is written
therein: for then thou shalt make thy
way prosperous, and then thou shalt
have good success."*

Money…people lie, cheat, steal and kill for it.

The price for prosperity in the World's economy is very high. But if you have knowledge from the Word and God given understanding, you will see that the cost of this prosperous and successful life in God's economy is found in *Joshua 1:8*…
(1) Speak God's Word.
(2) Meditate on God's Word.
(3) Do "all" that is written in the Word.

When you do these things, prosperity and success will follow you. Remember this, God doesn't bless your ignorance, He blesses your knowledge, your understanding and your diligence.

*Luke 6:38, "Give, and it shall be
given unto you, good measure,
pressed down, and shaken together,
and running over shall men give into
your bosom. For with the same
measure that you mete withal it shall
be measured to you again."*

TITHING IS THE KEY TO YOUR SOWING BEING BLESSED.

Malachi 3:10 – 11, "Bring ye all the tithes into the storehouse, that there may be meat in mine house, and prove me now herewith, saith the LORD of hosts, if I will not open you the windows of Heaven, and pour you out a blessing that there shall not be room enough to receive it. And I will rebuke the devourer for your sakes, and he shall not destroy the fruits of your ground, neither shall your vine cast her fruit before the time in the field, saith the LORD of hosts."

Tithing is not sowing. Tithing is your obedience to God's commands. Tithing is returning to God what is already His. You tithe God's 10%, then you sow from your 90%. But please remember this, your faithful tithing is the key to Gods great blessings resting upon the seed you are sowing, and the great harvest you will receive.

REAPING A HARVEST IS NOT AUTOMATIC.

Some think reaping a harvest is automatic. Now the growing is automatic, but the reaping is not. God grows the farmers crop, but the farmer must go into the field to bring in the harvest. Do you remember when God sent manna for His people, but the children of Israel had to go collect it? They could not just sit in the tent and make good confessions; they had to go and reap it.

QUESTIONS FOR YOU TO ANSWER.

1.   Do you know how much you sowed above your tithe last year? If you do not know how much seed you sowed, then you do not know how to believe for and expect a great multiplied harvest.
2.   Did you sow into good ground? Sow into ministries like this one that have a vision and are on a mission to provide the Gospel to those who have not yet come to Christ.
3.   Do you believe in a 30-fold or 50-fold return on your sowing? Let's look at the natural example of the harvest.

A NATURAL EXAMPLE OF SOWING AND REAPING.

If you plant a bushel of wheat per acre, you get a yield of 40 to 60 bushels an acre in a good year. This is a 40%-60% return on the seeds sown.

Plant a bushel of soybeans to an acre and you will see a yield of about 30-50 bushels an acre in a good year.

If you would plant just 1/3 of a bushel of corn to an acre, in a good year you would have a yield of 100-150 bushels an acre. This is a 333% to 500% return.

EXPECT A BIG HARVEST.

In the natural we expect big returns. It works the same way in God's financial harvest as well. Are you really expecting your return? Have you sowed above your tithe? Have you stirred up your faith to believe for this kind of return? It is the exercise of your faith that brings in the harvest. Small faith and little sowing combine to make a small harvest. It's time to rethink our ideas about spiritual sowing and reaping. We must keep expecting and keep sowing and expecting and sowing and expecting…

THE RULES FOR YOUR FINANCIAL BLESSING ARE IN THE WORD!

Think the Word
Speak the Word
Live the Word

Joshua 1:8 explains how important this is:

> *"This book of the law shall not depart out of thy mouth, but thou shalt meditate therein day and night, that thou mayest observe to do according to all that is written therein: for then thou shalt make thy way prosperous, and then thou shalt have good success."*

There are unbiblical doctrines that say... people are in poverty because God is trying to teach them something. God does not teach you through lack and poverty and sickness. He is the great provider. He is the source of all good things. God wants you to have the very best that this world has to offer.

AND FINALLY...

1. _GOD WANTS TO BLESS YOU SO YOU CAN HELP OTHERS._

Jesus told us when we help the disenfranchised, the poor and needy; we are doing the work of God. God is looking for those with giving hearts.

> _Matthew 25:40, "Inasmuch as ye have done it unto one of the least of these my brethren, ye have done in unto me."_

2. _HE WANTS TO BLESS YOU SO YOU CAN HELP SEND HIS WORD TO THOSE WHO HAVEN'T HEARD._

We are blessed to be a blessing. God has given you everything you have so you can be a giver. We must not consume all His blessings upon our own desires and wants. We must be willing to share His blessings with those who are in need.

> _Romans 10:15, "And how shall they preach unless they are sent? As it is written, "how beautiful are the feet of those who preach the gospel of peace, who bring glad tidings of good things!"_

3. GOD WANTS TO BLESS YOU SO YOU CAN RETURN THE TITHE AND SOW INTO THE KINGDOM OF GOD FOR A GREAT HARVEST.

What would happen if you began receiving more money and things than you knew what to do with? Would you be surprised? You shouldn't be. God has promised some powerful blessings to those who will follow His plan. Your faithful tithing and sowing give God the right and responsibility to rebuke the devourer and pour blessings into your life. When you give you can expect a harvest from God.

> *Malachi 3: 10-11, "Bring ye all the tithes into the storehouse, that there may be meat in mine house, and prove me now herewith, saith the LORD of hosts, if I will not open you the windows of Heaven, and pour you out a blessing that there shall not be room enough to receive it. And I will rebuke the devourer for your sakes, and he shall not destroy the fruits of your ground, neither shall your vine cast her fruit before the time in the field, saith the LORD of hosts."*

Luke 6:38, "Give, and you will receive. Your gift will return to you in full – pressed down, shaken together to make room for more, running over, and poured into your lap. The amount you give will determine the amount you get back."

4. HE WANTS TO BLESS YOU SO YOU CAN PROVIDE FOR YOUR LOVED ONES.

God wants you to have enough finances to bless your family. He wants you to succeed and have the best of His provision.

1 Timothy 5:8, "But if anyone does not provide for his own, and especially for those of his household, he has denied the faith and is worse than an unbeliever."

God desires to bless you. He gets no glory from your lack and poverty, your sickness and disease, your defeat and loss.

Matthew 7:11, "If you then, being evil, know how to give good gifts to your children, how much more will your Father who is in Heaven give good things to those who ask Him!"

5. GOD WILL BLESS YOU AND REVEAL THE LOCATION OF YOUR SUPERNATURAL FINANCIAL PROVISIONS TO YOU

Remember this…God does not need to create anything new to supply every need that you have. He has already provided everything you need to succeed in this world. Faith reaches up into His provision (already available) and pulls it into your life. As you seek Him and stay in His Word He will reveal where to find the provision and how to receive it.

> *Philippians 4:19, "But my God shall supply all your need according to His riches in glory by Christ Jesus."*

> *1 Kings 17: 3-4, "Get away from here and turn eastward, and hide by the brook Cherith, which flows into the Jordan. And it will be that you shall drink from the brook, and I have commanded the ravens to feed you there."*

6. *GOD IS GOOD ALL THE TIME AND HE WANTS TO BLESS YOU*

Remember this, God is good all the time and the devil is bad all the time. There is no agreement between God and the devil to teach us lessons through sickness, disease, pain, trouble, depression, lack and poverty. These things are the works of the devil himself, Satan sends fires and floods, sickness, disease and death. God brings salvation, deliverance, healing life and joy!

> **John 10:10, "The thief does not come except to steal, and to kill, and to destroy. I have come that they may have life, and that they may have it more abundantly."**

7. *KNOW THE WORD AND GET WISDOM*

Your knowledge and understanding of the Word used skillfully will bring wisdom. Wisdom will change things in your life! You don't have to be defeated! You don't have to be depressed!

> **Proverbs 3:13, "Blessed is the man who finds wisdom, the man who gains understanding."**

Proverbs 4:7, "Wisdom is the most important thing: so get wisdom. If it costs everything you have, get understanding."

8. YOU ARE RIGHTEOUS IN HIM

You are the righteousness of God in Christ... a joint heir with Jesus!

Romans 3:22, "Even the righteousness of God which is by faith of Jesus Christ unto all and upon all them that believe."

You are Saved...by His righteousness.
You are Healed...by His righteousness.
You are Delivered...by His righteousness.
You are Made rich...by His righteousness.

Because of a Godly "righteousness transfusion" into your life, your faith will work every time...in every area of your life...for trouble, salvation, sickness, finances... Every problem is the same to God!

9.   _DO NOT COMPLAIN, STAY IN FAITH_

The children of Israel failed many times in the wilderness…they murmured and complained, and I believe that's why they were there so long. We must refuse to follow the example of the wilderness experience. Do not murmur, do not complain.

We must stay in an environment of faith and praise with no complaining. We need Faith associations…Faith teaching…Faith friends…

We need Faith people, to help us get stronger in faith. We need to encourage one another.

10. _YOU ARE VICTORIOUS_

God's ways will bring you up and out…man's ways will take you back to Egypt! The devil wants you to see yourself broke, sick, lost and defeated. But God sees you rich, healed, healthy, saved and victorious. _**"I've never seen the righteous forsaken or his seed begging for bread." Psalm 37:25.**_

Believers are not beggars! You are God's best!

You are His chosen! When you see yourself as God sees you...the righteousness of God in Christ, you will be filled with faith. You will become bold! You will be able to take on every attack of the enemy. The Word of God will defeat the devil. Your faith will bring you victory.

The Legacy of Gary McSpadden

Gary's Legacy

Was that his life would inspire others with love and kindness building a life of faith and wisdom.

Celebrating Gary's life with words from family and friends

Family and Friends

Words spoken by family and friends to give honor, love, and inspiration to those who read this book.

Wonderful memories to celebrate a purpose filled life of serving his Lord and Savior. The focus of his life!

Matthew 25:21   2 Timothy 4-7

Epilogue

In Remembrance

These words are of those closest to Gary McSpadden, testimonials of the great man of God he was in our lives.

Carol McSpadden:

Bride of Gary McSpadden

Gary was the strength of our family and was led by the Holy Spirit to give Words of Wisdom to our children and grandchildren as they faced problems in growing up.

He was a teacher at heart and always loved helping others in time of need, quoting scriptures from the Bible and spiritual advice that the anointing would place within him.

Gary was a loving husband, father, grandfather and loved by so many as a caring Pastor of Faith & Wisdom Church.

His greatest desire was to see the very best in every person and help them to grow and know God in a personal way through Salvation. He was a wonderful man of God!

He was blessed with many gifts, a man with a beautiful voice and sang with many groups such as Oak Ridge Quartet, Imperials, Bill Gaither Trio, Gaither Vocal Band and recorded many great albums. He was a song writer, publisher, speaker and artist who appeared on many TV programs around the world. God blessed him tremendously, never asking, but through God's blessings, doors were always opened to him to minister and spread the Gospel.

Gary was always a minister at heart! His concerts were always music and Ministry combined. His motivation was to encourage people, love them and present Salvation to bring them to the Lord. He was a preacher and teacher at heart, which led to the beginning of Faith & Wisdom Church in 2005 as a prayer group with a few people in our home. After a few years the church grew to several hundred and continued to build to a great church today.

The book FAITH WORKS came from his heart and the anointed Word of God. Put FAITH to work, apply to your life and everyday living and you will see God do amazing changes and miracles in all you do.

Use these words of FAITH every day! Read them, memorize them and put them in your heart.

<u>Speak Them Out Daily</u>. God's Promise is TRUTH! He will NEVER leave you or forsake you.

FAITH will strengthen you and make you strong to face all the devil brings against you.

My FAITH has led me through all I have gone through these last few years. God has made me a stronger person and a stronger Christian to help other ladies to get through these same situations. Praise the Lord for leading me by FAITH in Him!

Gary was and is the love of my life, Forever!

Shawn McSpadden:
Son of Gary McSpadden

I grew up in a household of Faith! My PaPa Mac and my Father were both men of Extreme Faith. At an early age, I remember being told Faith is stepping out and standing on nothing until it became something. Whew!! That can be tough in a world that tells us the exact opposite on a daily basis. Believe in only yourself, don't trust anyone, "seeing is believing" is how the world responds but the Bible teaches that we must trust and have Faith in the things unseen. It is through discipline and prayer that our Faith grows.

As we submit to our Heavenly Father He says He will provide for us, all we have to do is commit and have Faith, not only is He faithful but His Word is faithful to us. This is completely counter to what the world tells us.

I know as I have lived on the words my Dad taught me, God has been faithful even when I haven't. The Lord continues to show up for me and in my life in ways that only He can. I have to daily step out and stand on nothing knowing it will become something and when it does you have to give God the glory because you know it was not you. When God does something you know it!!! You had nothing and now God has given you something from His gracefulness and mercy.

The only reason this happens is because His nature is to be faithful. He does not know how to be anything else. So when you do not have the answers and need Him, step out, pray, believe and stand firm in the Word knowing God will show up for you like He has in His Word hundreds of times for all the men and women who believed.

So today step out and stand firm knowing God is the only one who will show up and honor your faithfulness in Him. These are words I hear from a loving Dad who loved a life of Faith. I miss you and love you for instilling this in me and our family.

Michelle Smith:

Daughter of Gary McSpadden

My Father was a man of faith! He loved to sing about it, preach about it and most of all share it with others. I have so many wonderful memories of his incredible life but the ones I will cherish the most are the many times I watched him reading his Bible and praying for our family and others. I am thankful for his life and even more thankful that he showed me what real faith was so I could make it on my own...

Thanks Daddy...it will never be the same again.

Ron Smith:

Son-in-Law of Gary McSpadden

I met my Father-in-law for the first time almost 40 years ago. In those decades of friendship and the many times he mentored me I never left an encounter with him that I was not lifted in my walk with Christ. He truly was a man of faith. In a very dark moment in my life he could have easily turned his back on me but instead he chose to love me and again help me walk in faith and seek the forgiveness that was available to me. He forgave me before anyone else did and his words helped heal a broken person. Simply put, I loved and still love him...I can only imagine what his homecoming was like as he saw how faith lived out can earn an incredible reward...I love you Gary.

Cheryl Kartsonakis:

Sister of Gary McSpadden

Gary was always my Big Brother. He was always there to protect me from many disasters in our childhood days of growing up. I loved and respected him as a fine Christian through his life of Ministry and I miss him so very much today! Gary could play many musical instruments: organ, alto sax, xylophone and usually whatever he picked up. As his little sister I just loved to sing harmony with him. Our parents had a radio program and Gary and I sang duets on that program! Gary with his strong and beautiful voice began to minister and sing with his ministry friend Claude Causey who was also a Minister.

After many years passed, and much prayer, the time came when God called Gary & Carol back into Ministry and they began Faith & Wisdom Church in Branson, Missouri. As my Pastors I admired and prayed for them as they were filled with the love of God and taught others so much of the love of God!

Dino Kartsonakis:

Brother-in-Law of Gary McSpadden

My brother-in-law Gary McSpadden was an amazing man, not only as a vocalist but also as my Pastor. His teaching of the Word has had a profound impact on my life. I miss him so much, but it won't be long until we meet again!

Gerry & Tammi Spicer:

Beloved friends of Gary McSpadden

We were privileged to work with Gary McSpadden at Faith & Wisdom Church for over 10 years. He was both our Pastor and friend. His daily walk with the Lord, his speech, attitude and love for others were inspiring. FAITH Works Now is a triumph for daily living. He would tell you that with Faith in God, nothing in your life is impossible. His legacy lives on in the pages of this book. It will bless your life, as knowing Gary has blessed ours.

www.ingramcontent.com/pod-product-compliance
Lightning Source LLC
Chambersburg PA
CBHW061713120626
46550CB00003B/1207